Sports Build Character
RESPONSIBILITY IN SPORTS

by Todd Kortemeier

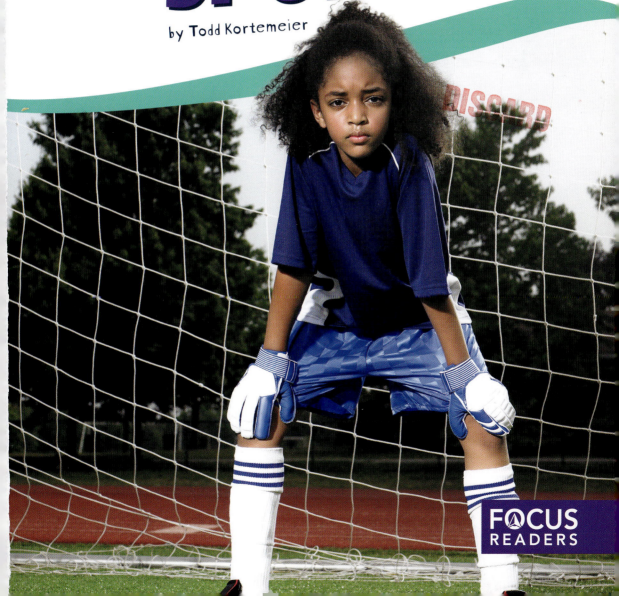

FOCUS READERS

www.focusreaders.com

Focus Readers is distributed by North Star Editions:
sales@northstareditions.com | 888-417-0195

Produced for Focus Readers by Red Line Editorial.

Photographs ©: Image Source/iStockphoto, cover, 1; asiseeit/iStockphoto, 4–5; PetePattavina/iStockphoto, 7; Kevork Djansezian/AP Images, 8–9; Marcio Jose Sanchez/AP Images, 11; Marcello Pozzetti/IPS Photo Agency/MAXPPP/Newscom, 12; Scott Heppell/AP Images, 14; Stephen Morton/AP Images, 16, 18; James D. Smith/AP Images, 20; DragonImages/iStockphoto, 22–23; viafilms/iStockphoto, 25; andresr/iStockphoto, 26–27, 29

ISBN
978-1-63517-535-6 (hardcover)
978-1-63517-607-0 (paperback)
978-1-63517-751-0 (ebook pdf)
978-1-63517-679-7 (hosted ebook)

Library of Congress Control Number: 2017948111

Printed in the United States of America
Mankato, MN
November, 2017

About the Author

Todd Kortemeier is a writer and editor from Minneapolis. He has written more than 50 books for young people, primarily on sports topics.

TABLE OF CONTENTS

CHAPTER 1

WHAT IS RESPONSIBILITY?

Every person is in charge of his or her own behavior. Nobody can make someone act a certain way. It is up to each person to do the right thing. Doing the right thing is the meaning of responsibility.

Golfers are responsible for taking care of their clubs.

It isn't always easy to be responsible. Sometimes the right thing is hard to do. It may require bravery.

Moments like these happen all the time in sports. In competitions, athletes must keep their heads in the game. There is often little time to prepare. Responsibility has to

LET'S DISCUSS

What are some examples of things you are responsible for?

 Catchers show responsibility by staying in position.

become a **habit**. Then an athlete

will be ready to act.

Responsibility is a **solo** task. But

it benefits everybody.

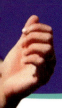

CHAPTER 2

RESPONSIBILITY IN ACTION

The 1999 Women's World Cup came down to **penalty kicks**. The United States was playing China in the final game. Neither team had scored a goal in 120 minutes of action.

US player Brandi Chastain celebrates during the 1999 Women's World Cup.

9

US player Brandi Chastain had been in this position before. Months earlier, she had missed a penalty kick against China. Since then, she had worked hard to improve her skill.

Chastain's coach noticed she could take kicks with either foot. He called on her to take the final kick against China. If she made it, her team would be world champions. Chastain was not nervous. She wanted the responsibility.

Chastain joined the National Soccer Hall of Fame in 2017.

Normally, Chastain used her right foot. But her coach suggested she use her left. It was enough to fool the goalie. The ball flew into the net. Chastain's hard work had paid off.

 Petr Cech is one of the best goalkeepers in the English Premier League.

Soccer may not be a high-contact sport. But it can still be dangerous.

Players vying for the ball can end up hurting one another.

In 2006, Chelsea goalkeeper Petr Cech was about to grab the ball. It was an easy play. But a player from the other team was running toward him. After Cech got the ball, the other player kneed him in the head.

Cech was down for several minutes. Medical professionals took him off the field on a **stretcher**. Cech had to go to the hospital. He needed emergency brain surgery.

Sometimes, Cech wears a face mask in addition to his helmet.

Cech's skull had been **fractured**. He nearly died.

Cech recovered after three months. When he returned, he wore a protective helmet on his head. He continued to wear it during every game he played. Cech suffered another blow in 2011. He said the helmet kept him safe.

Cech's helmet makes it tough to hear his teammates. But he shows responsibility by keeping himself safe. The helmet is what allows him to keep playing.

LET'S DISCUSS

What are some examples of actions you take to stay safe?

Davis (left) speaks with the tour director after his failed swing.

Brian Davis was tired of second place. The golfer had finished in second place three times in his career. He hadn't won a single tournament yet. At the 2010

Verizon Heritage, Davis looked like he might finally break through.

Davis and Jim Furyk were tied after 72 holes. They went to a playoff. The golfer to win a hole first would win the tournament. On the first hole, Davis was trying to **chip** onto the **green**.

As he swung the club back, he clipped a loose branch. Nobody else saw it. It had no effect on his swing. But Davis noticed it. And he knew it was against the rules.

Furyk celebrates his close win.

Davis called out his mistake, even though that wasn't his job. Officials looked at a replay. Using slow motion, they saw Davis's mistake. It was a two-**stroke** penalty. Davis knew that made the hole almost impossible to win. He decided to **concede** the tournament to Furyk.

Davis had to settle for another second-place finish. But his show of responsibility earned him much respect on the tour.

LET'S DISCUSS

Why do you think Davis called the penalty if nobody else saw it?

 Dak Prescott shows responsibility on and off the field.

Dallas Cowboys quarterback Dak Prescott is usually a good passer. But in a 2017 game, he missed the trashcan with his empty water cup.

A football bench is a messy place. Players often toss their trash on the ground. Fans do the same in the stands.

But Prescott got off the bench and threw his cup away. He didn't think it was a big deal. Putting trash in the trashcan was natural to him. But this small gesture showed Prescott was responsible for his actions.

LET'S DISCUSS

How do you show responsibility each day?

CHAPTER 3

RESPONSIBILITY AND YOU

Nobody else can be responsible for you. Responsibility is something you must do yourself. Teammates count on one another in sports. In everyday life, your friends and family are counting on you, too.

Owning sports equipment requires responsibility.

Responsibility usually comes down to small things. It means doing what you are supposed to do. And it means doing so without being asked.

Showing responsibility means that you are reliable. Others know that you will not let them down. Being responsible prepares you for

LET'S DISCUSS

What do you think happens when people are irresponsible?

 Families can show responsibility by recycling paper and plastic.

whatever happens next. This comes

in handy both on and off the field.

ARE YOU RESPONSIBLE?

Ask yourself these questions and decide.

- Do I know what is expected of me?
- Do I do what I say I'm going to do?
- Do I always try my best?
- Do I admit when I'm wrong?
- Do I try to fix my mistakes?

Responsibility is a full-time job. But it doesn't mean being perfect. Challenge yourself today to do one responsible act. You could clean your room. Or you could help cook dinner.

Saving your money is an example of responsibility.

FOCUS ON
RESPONSIBILITY

Write your answers on a separate piece of paper.

1. Write a one-sentence summary of how Brandi Chastain showed responsibility in Chapter 2.

2. If you were Petr Cech, would you keep playing with the helmet? Why or why not?

3. In which year did Petr Cech fracture his skull?
     A. 1999
     B. 2006
     C. 2011

4. Why did Dak Prescott throw away his empty water cup?
     A. to keep the bench clean
     B. to practice his throw
     C. to receive attention from fans

5. What does **vying** mean in this book?

*Soccer may not be a high-contact sport. But it can still be dangerous. Players **vying** for the ball can end up hurting one another.*

    A. injuring
    B. competing
    C. touching

6. What does **gesture** mean in this book?

*Putting trash in the trashcan was natural to him. But this small **gesture** showed Prescott was responsible for his actions.*

    A. action
    B. number
    C. belief

Answer key on page 32.

GLOSSARY

chip
In golf, a short shot meant to reach the green.

concede
To give victory to an opponent.

fractured
Broken or cracked.

green
In golf, the area of grass surrounding the hole.

habit
Something that someone does regularly.

penalty kicks
Free kicks in soccer that a player takes alone against the goalkeeper.

solo
Doing something alone.

stretcher
A medical device used to carry sick or injured people.

stroke
A swing of the club in golf.

TO LEARN MORE

BOOKS

Herzog, Brad. *Inspiring Stories of Sportsmanship.* Minneapolis: Free Spirit Publishing, 2014.

Kurtz, Kevin. *What Makes Sports Gear Safer?* Minneapolis: Lerner Publications, 2016.

Nelson, Robin. *Can People Count on Me? A Book about Responsibility.* Minneapolis: Lerner Publications, 2014.

NOTE TO EDUCATORS

Visit **www.focusreaders.com** to find lesson plans, activities, links, and other resources related to this title.

INDEX

Answer Key: 1. Answers will vary; **2.** Answers will vary; **3.** B; **4.** A; **5.** B; **6.** A